AI and You: Thriving in the Era of Artificial Intelligence is a practical guide designed to help readers understand and adapt to AI's growing presence in the workplace, education, and daily life. The book demystifies AI concepts, highlights its transformative potential, and provides actionable strategies for leveraging AI tools while addressing challenges like job displacement, bias, and privacy concerns. Emphasizing adaptability, continuous learning, and a balanced approach, it empowers readers to embrace AI as a tool for personal and professional growth while contributing to its responsible and ethical use in society.

About the Author

Dr. Elias Aydi is an Assistant Professor of Physics and Astronomy at Texas Tech University. Dr. Aydi's research focuses on exploring transient astronomical phenomena, particularly novae. His work has significantly advanced the understanding of these explosive events. As part of being an astrophysicist, Dr. Aydi uses coding significantly in his work and lately he has been lured by the world of Artificial Intelligence and its application in both scientific research and real life. Apart from working in research, Dr. Aydi is passionate about science communication and public engagement, aspiring to bridge the gaps between scientists and the public.

Table of content:

Introduction: The AI Revolution is Here

- **What is AI?**

Artificial intelligence (AI) refers to computer systems designed to perform tasks that traditionally require human intelligence. These tasks include recognizing speech, understanding natural language, making decisions, and even solving problems. While AI might sound futuristic, it's already an integral part of our everyday lives, often in ways we may not realize.

Take, for example, self-driving cars. These vehicles use AI to analyze data from cameras, radar, and sensors in real-time. This enables them to recognize objects like pedestrians, traffic signs, and other vehicles, allowing them to navigate roads safely without human intervention. Companies like Tesla and Waymo are leading the charge, showing us how AI can transform transportation and make it more efficient.

Chatbots are another widespread use of AI. You've likely interacted with one when contacting customer support online. AI-powered chatbots can understand and respond to customer queries using natural language processing (NLP), a branch of AI focused on interpreting human language. For instance, platforms like ChatGPT and virtual assistants like Siri and Alexa can hold conversations, answer questions, and even execute commands, saving us time and effort.

Facial recognition is yet another application of AI that many encounter daily, often through smartphones. Unlocking a phone with a face scan relies on AI algorithms to analyze and match facial features. Beyond personal devices, facial recognition is used in security systems, airports, and even retail stores to improve safety and efficiency.

These examples illustrate how AI systems are designed to replicate human abilities but often surpass human performance in speed, scale, and precision. Whether helping us navigate, communicate, or secure our information, AI is reshaping how we interact with technology and the world around us. The more we understand these capabilities, the better we can harness them to improve our lives.

What is the difference between AI, Machine Learning, and deep learning? AI, machine learning (ML), and deep learning (DL) are closely related, but they aren't the same thing. AI is the broad concept of creating machines or systems that can simulate human intelligence, such as reasoning, problem-solving, and decision-making. Within AI, machine learning is a specific subset that focuses on teaching machines to learn patterns from data and improve their performance over time without being explicitly programmed. For example, a machine learning algorithm might analyze thousands of email examples to learn how to distinguish between spam and legitimate messages. Deep learning, on the other hand, is a specialized branch of machine learning that uses artificial neural networks inspired by the structure of the human brain. These networks are particularly powerful for tasks like recognizing images or understanding speech. While AI is the overarching field, machine learning and deep learning are the techniques driving many of the most advanced AI applications today.

- **Why This Book?**

In a TV interview aired in 1995 as part of the Letterman show, David Letterman taunt Bill Gates about this new concept called the *internet*, where Gates try to explain to Letterman the benefits of this new tool while Letterman jokingly brush it off as a useless invention! The interview goes as follow:

Letterman: "What about this internet thing? Do you know anything about that?"

Gates: "Sure".

Letterman: "What the hell is that exactly?"

Gates: "It's become a place where people are publishing information. Everybody can have their own homepage, companies are there, the latest information. It's wild what is going on. You can send electronic mail to people. It is the big new thing."

Letterman: "Yeah, it is easy to criticize something you don't fully understand, which is my position here, but I can remember a couple of months ago, there was like a big breakthrough announcement that on the internet or on some computer deal, they were going to broadcast a baseball game. You could listen to a baseball game on your computer. And I just thought to myself, does radio ring a bell? You know what I mean?"

Gates replies while laughing: "there is a difference. You can listen to the baseball game whenever you want."

Letterman: "Do tape recorders ring a bell?"

They both laugh! Of course, we won't go through the entire interview here, but we all know what happened just 10 years later with the internet. Now, 30 years later, the internet is not just an integral part of our lives, but it is becoming for a lot of people life itself (talk about people who literally spend more time online than doing anything else). AI now is like the internet in 1995, but the only difference is that no one dares to question its usefulness, because we are now all aware how inventions and developments like this are taking over our lives rapidly. AI is already playing a key role in our daily lives, and we can only imagine what the case will be by the end of the decade or in 10 years from now. Therefore, understanding AI and harnessing its power is your future toolbox as I elaborate further below.

AI, the next internet. Understanding AI is essential for everyone because it is no longer just a tool for tech experts – it is a transformative force shaping nearly every aspect of our lives. AI is revolutionizing industries, changing how we work, learn, and interact. Jobs across sectors, from healthcare to finance to retail, increasingly rely on AI-powered tools to streamline processes, analyze data, and deliver personalized experiences. For example, medical professionals use AI to detect diseases more accurately, while financial analysts use it to identify market trends. Workers who understand how to leverage these tools are more likely to stay competitive in their careers.

In education, AI is personalizing learning experiences for students of all ages. Platforms like Duolingo and Khan Academy adapt to individual learning styles and paces, making education more effective and accessible. AI also helps educators by automating tasks such as grading and tracking student progress, allowing them to focus more on teaching and mentoring.

In daily life, AI touches everything from the way we communicate to how we shop and entertain ourselves. Virtual assistants like Alexa and Google Assistant help manage tasks, while recommendation systems on platforms like Netflix or Spotify tailor content to our preferences. By understanding AI, people can make informed decisions about how to use these technologies responsibly and effectively.

As AI becomes more embedded in society, understanding it is no longer optional. It empowers individuals to navigate changes, seize opportunities, and address challenges such as data privacy and ethical considerations. Knowing how AI works, and its implications, ensures that people remain active participants in shaping the future rather than passive observers of technological change.

- **What You'll Learn?**

This book will guide you through the transformative world of artificial intelligence, starting with a clear explanation of AI concepts in everyday life, using relatable examples such as chatbots and self-driving cars. Readers will learn how AI is reshaping industries, from healthcare to education, and gain practical tips for adapting to these changes, including leveraging AI tools for productivity and personal growth. Case studies of individuals and organizations thriving in the AI era will provide real-world insights, while curated resources, such as online courses, AI-powered apps, and community forums, will equip readers to continue their learning journey. By the end, readers will have a comprehensive understanding of AI's role in their lives, actionable strategies to harness its benefits, and the confidence to navigate an AI-driven world with resilience and adaptability.

Part 1: Understanding AI in Everyday Life

1. AI in Your Pocket: Smartphones and Smart Assistants

AI powers tools like Siri, Alexa, and Google Assistant by enabling them to understand and respond to human language. These assistants use a branch of AI called natural language processing (NLP) to interpret the words we speak or type. For example, when you ask, "What's the weather like today?" the AI breaks your question into smaller parts, analyzes the meaning, and determines that you're looking for weather information. It then connects to a database or online service to retrieve the relevant information and responds to you in a conversational way. This ability to understand context and provide meaningful answers makes these tools feel like they're truly intelligent.

Beyond simple questions, these assistants also use AI to learn and adapt to your preferences. Over time, they might recognize your favorite songs, frequently visited locations, or daily routines, offering personalized suggestions or reminders. For instance, Alexa might recommend a playlist you like during your usual workout time, or Google Assistant could remind you to leave early for an appointment based on traffic conditions. These tools combine AI's ability to process data, recognize patterns, and predict needs to make our lives more convenient and efficient.

To get the most out of AI tools like Siri and Alexa, start by customizing their settings to match your preferences and needs. Train the assistant to recognize your voice for personalized responses and enable features like routines or shortcuts to automate frequent tasks. For instance, you can set up a morning routine where Alexa turns on the lights, reads the weather, and starts your favorite playlist with a single command. Regularly updating the software ensures you're benefiting from the latest features and improvements. Additionally, explore integrations with other smart devices or apps to create a more connected and efficient experience in managing your daily activities.

While these tools can enhance convenience, it's important to address privacy concerns. Review and adjust the privacy settings in the companion app to control how your data is collected and stored. For example, you can disable the saving of voice recordings or set preferences for when the assistant listens. Be mindful of sharing sensitive information via these devices and consider using features like voice recognition to prevent unauthorized access. Periodically delete stored data, such as voice history, to minimize risks. By balancing optimization with mindful privacy practices, you can fully enjoy the benefits of AI tools while protecting your personal information.

Your phones are also packed with AI tools, all inside your side pocket. And it is just the start! AI is expected to play an integral part in phone designs and software. Our smartphones use AI to make everyday tasks easier, faster, and more personalized. While AI tools like the ones discussed above (e.g., Siri and Google Assistant) are all now a key part of a smartphone, AI features are taking over the smartphone world. Using AI, our phone cameras can automatically adjust settings for better photos and even recognize faces to organize your photo library. AI improves typing with predictive text and autocorrect, suggesting the next word or fixing errors as you type. Apps like Google Maps use AI to provide real-time traffic updates and suggest the fastest routes. Even your favorite streaming or shopping apps use AI to recommend content or products based on your preferences. By quietly working in the background, AI makes smartphones smarter and more intuitive to use.

2. AI at Home: Smart Homes and Entertainment

A scenario of what your day might look like, in the *not very far* future:

As the sun begins to rise, your smart curtains gently open to let in natural light, while your AI-driven thermostat adjusts the temperature to your preferred cozy morning warmth. The kitchen springs to life: your coffee maker brews your favorite blend, and the fridge suggests breakfast options based on what's inside. As you head to the bathroom, the mirror displays a personalized morning briefing – weather, news, and your schedule – all curated by AI systems that know your habits better than you do. Throughout the day, the AI in your home anticipates your needs. It dims the lights and starts your relaxation playlist when you settle into the living room after work. Your security system keeps watch, not just for intruders but for deliveries, notifying you when a package arrives and even unlocking the door for the courier. Your TV starts playing your favorite program, which you enjoy watching after a long day of work. In the evening the TV plays your favorite genre of documentaries without you even browsing – it is trying to help you wind down and relax before a good night sleep. The system seems to understand you on a deeply personal level, offering recommendations and adjustments that make your life smoother and more enjoyable.

AI is transforming our homes by making everyday gadgets smarter, more efficient, and easier to use. AI-driven thermostats, like Nest, learn your habits over time to automatically adjust the temperature based on your preferences. For example, they might lower the heat at night when you're sleeping and warm up your home just before you wake up, saving energy while keeping you comfortable. Smart lighting systems, like Philips Hue, can be controlled with your voice or an app, letting you change brightness or color and even set schedules. Some systems use AI to sense when you enter or leave a room and adjust the lights, accordingly, adding convenience and reducing energy waste. AI-powered security cameras, such as Ring or Arlo, go beyond recording footage; they can detect motion, recognize faces, and send alerts to your phone if something unusual happens, giving you peace of mind even when you're not home.

In the future, AI at home is expected to become even more advanced. Smart devices will become better at working together, creating a truly connected home. For example, your thermostat could communicate with your lighting system and blinds to maintain the perfect indoor environment based on weather and sunlight. AI will also enhance personalization, understanding your daily routines in greater detail to anticipate your needs, like brewing your coffee when you wake up or turning on calming music after a long day. Additionally, voice assistants will become more conversational and intuitive, making it easier to manage your home with natural, everyday language. As AI continues to evolve, homes will not only be more efficient and secure but also tailored to create a truly comfortable and stress-free living experience.

But as the AI's presence grows, so does its reach into your privacy. Your voice assistant listens all the time, even when you don't activate it, picking up on private conversations. The fridge tracks your eating habits and shares that data with advertisers, suddenly bombarding you with promotions for diet plans. The security cameras not only keep your home safe but also analyze your behavior and share it with third-party companies, all in the name of "improving your experience." *One evening, while relaxing on the couch, you wonder how much of your life is truly private anymore.*

The convenience is undeniable – your home feels almost magical, anticipating your needs at every turn. But the subtle trade-off of your personal information for this comfort starts to weigh on you. It's a world where AI has optimized everything, but the question remains: how much of your autonomy and privacy are you willing to give up for the sake of ease? This future may be luxurious, but it reminds us to think critically about the balance between convenience and control.

Balancing the convenience of AI-driven home gadgets with data privacy is essential to enjoy the benefits of smart technology without compromising your personal information. Here are a few tips that helps you to reach that balance:

- Most smart devices allow you to control how much data they collect and share. For instance, you can disable features like voice recording history or location tracking in your smart assistant. Adjusting these settings ensures the device works for you without unnecessarily invading your privacy.
- Only share data with devices when it's absolutely necessary. For example, if your AI assistant offers to personalize services by storing your voice commands,

consider whether you truly need this feature. Opt-out of data sharing programs when possible.

- Use a strong, encrypted Wi-Fi connection and separate your smart devices on a guest network. This reduces the risk of all your devices being compromised if one is hacked.
- Regularly check what data your devices have collected and delete it if it's unnecessary. Many smart assistants and gadgets allow you to review and erase stored voice recordings, search histories, or activity logs.
- While integrating multiple devices can enhance convenience, it also creates more points of vulnerability. Only connect gadgets that are essential to your lifestyle and ensure each one has strong privacy settings.
- Make sure everyone in your household understands how to use the devices securely. Teach them about privacy settings and safe practices, like not sharing sensitive information with AI assistants.

By taking these precautions, you can enjoy the convenience of AI at home while maintaining control over your personal data and privacy. Remember, the key is to stay informed and proactive about how your gadgets operate and what data they access.

Many people wonder; even if I do all the above, what if the developers of these smart devices did not adhere to their privacy policies? Can we trust that these companies are obeying the rule? Well, here comes the role of the decision makers in forcing these companies to obey and adhere to their privacy policies. So, choose wisely when you are casting your votes in the next elections. You need to make sure that whoever you pick to be in decision making positions, should have a good understanding of the AI world and its implications on the lives of the citizens. The decision makers must be up to date with the latest developments in the field of technology and are not out of touch with where our future is heading.

3. AI in the Workplace

AI in the workplace is transforming how we work by making tasks faster, easier, and more efficient. Artificial intelligence is being used across industries to streamline processes, save time, and improve decision-making. From automating repetitive tasks to helping teams stay organized, AI tools are becoming essential in the modern workplace. By handling routine and time-consuming activities, AI allows people to focus on more creative, strategic, and meaningful work.

One way AI is used is through **automation software**, which handles repetitive tasks like data entry, invoice processing, or scheduling. For example, tools like Zapier and UiPath can automatically move information between apps, saving hours of manual work. In a busy office, this might mean automatically updating a spreadsheet every time a new email comes in or generating reports with the click of a button. This reduces errors and speeds up processes that once took hours.

Project management platforms powered by AI, like Asana or Monday.com, help teams stay organized and on track. These tools can prioritize tasks, send reminders, and even predict when projects are at risk of falling behind based on past performance. AI in project management doesn't just keep everyone on schedule – it also helps identify ways to work more efficiently, offering suggestions on how to allocate resources better or highlighting bottlenecks.

Chatbots are another popular AI tool in the workplace, especially in customer service. These bots can answer common questions, resolve issues, and even process orders without needing human intervention. For instance, when you message a company on their website or social media, the initial response often comes from an AI chatbot like Drift or Intercom. These bots save time for employees by handling simple tasks, leaving complex problems for human staff.

ChatGPT; I bet you have heard this word multiple times before. What is ChatGPT and other similar tools that are available to users nowadays? ChatGPT, an advanced AI language model, is a powerful tool for improving your work and productivity in numerous ways. It acts as a virtual assistant, helping with tasks that range from brainstorming ideas to drafting content, saving you time and effort. For example, if you're stuck on writing an email, creating a report, or generating creative ideas for a project, ChatGPT can provide well-structured suggestions or even full drafts, allowing you to focus on refining rather than starting from scratch.

One of its key benefits is its ability to provide quick access to information. Instead of searching through multiple sources, you can ask ChatGPT to summarize a topic, explain a concept, or outline steps for a task. This makes it an excellent tool for research or learning, especially when you need concise answers without sifting through lengthy materials. It can also help you create to-do lists, prioritize tasks, and set actionable goals, keeping your workflow organized and efficient.

Collaboration is another area where ChatGPT shines. It can serve as a sounding board for ideas, helping you refine strategies or explore alternative approaches to solving problems. For example, if you're planning a presentation or brainstorming marketing strategies, ChatGPT can generate options you might not have considered. It can also assist with editing and proofreading, ensuring your communication is clear and professional.

Additionally, ChatGPT is a great time-saver for repetitive or routine tasks. Whether it's drafting social media posts, creating templates, or responding to frequently asked questions, it handles these tasks quickly and accurately. By automating parts of your workload, you can focus your energy on higher-value activities that require your unique expertise and creativity.

In short, ChatGPT, and other AI language models like Gemini and Google Assistant, enhance productivity by streamlining tasks, providing instant insights, and supporting creativity. By integrating it into your workflow, you can work smarter, meet deadlines more efficiently, and free up time to focus on what matters most.

But the question that everyone keeps asking, how does ChatGPT work? Is it thinking and reasoning like a human being to give us rapid answers to our questions or to draft emails for us? ChatGPT and similar language models work by using artificial intelligence to understand and generate human-like text. These models are trained on massive amounts of text data, such as books, articles, and websites, to learn the patterns and relationships between words and phrases. Once trained, they can take a prompt or question from you, analyze it, and generate a response that feels natural and relevant. An easy way to understand how ChatGPT works is to think of it as a highly advanced version of predictive text on your smartphone. When you start typing a message, your phone suggests the next word based on what you've written so far. Similarly, ChatGPT predicts the next words in a sentence, but on a much larger scale. It doesn't suggest one word – it rather generates entire paragraphs or even pages of text that make sense based on the context of your input.

Another analogy is to imagine a very well-read person who has studied countless books and conversations. If you ask them a question or give them a topic, they can piece together an answer by recalling and combining what they've learned. However, unlike a human, ChatGPT doesn't truly "know" or "understand" things – it's simply recognizing patterns in the data it has been trained on and using those patterns to create a response. For example, if you ask ChatGPT for a recipe or help with writing an email, it looks at your request, finds patterns that match how recipes or emails are typically written, and creates a response based on that. It doesn't cook or send emails itself; it just generates text that fits the request. This ability to mimic human language makes it feel conversational and helpful, even though it's essentially a very sophisticated text generator.

In simple terms, ChatGPT is like a digital assistant that's really good at guessing what comes next in a conversation based on what it has "read" in the past. It can be incredibly useful for answering questions, solving problems, or generating ideas, but it's important to remember that it's not a human and doesn't think or reason the way we do.

The impact of AI on some industries.

AI has already transformed several industries by improving efficiency, accuracy, and personalization. Here's a closer look at how it's revolutionizing healthcare, finance, and retail:

Healthcare. AI in healthcare is saving lives and enhancing patient care. For example, AI-powered diagnostic tools analyze medical images, such as X-rays and MRIs, to detect diseases like cancer at an early stage with high accuracy. Tools like IBM's Watson Health assist doctors by analyzing massive datasets of medical research and patient records to recommend treatment options. In hospitals, AI streamlines administrative tasks like scheduling and billing, freeing up staff to focus on patient care. AI-driven apps also provide personalized health monitoring, such as wearable devices that track heart rates and alert users or doctors to potential health issues before they become critical.

The **finance** industry uses AI extensively to enhance decision-making and security. AI algorithms analyze market trends and predict stock movements, helping investors make informed decisions. In banking, AI-powered fraud detection systems monitor transactions in real-time, flagging suspicious activity and reducing the risk of fraud. Virtual assistants and chatbots are transforming customer service by helping clients check balances, process payments, and answer queries without needing a human representative. Additionally, AI is used to assess creditworthiness by analyzing more data points than traditional methods, enabling faster and fairer loan approvals.

In **retail**, AI is creating highly personalized shopping experiences. Online platforms like Amazon use AI to recommend products based on your browsing history and preferences. In physical stores, AI-powered inventory management systems predict demand and optimize stock levels, reducing waste and ensuring popular items are always available. Chatbots assist shoppers by answering questions and guiding them through the purchase process. Retailers also use AI in marketing, analyzing customer behavior to create targeted campaigns that resonate with specific audiences. Advanced tools like cashier-less stores (e.g., Amazon Go) use AI to track what customers pick up and charge them automatically, eliminating checkout lines.

These examples highlight how AI is transforming industries by automating processes, improving decision-making, and enhancing the customer experience. As AI continues to advance, its impact will only grow, reshaping more industries and creating new opportunities for innovation.

Overall, AI tools are reshaping workplaces by improving productivity and creating smoother workflows. Whether it's automating repetitive tasks, keeping teams organized, or providing instant customer support, AI allows businesses to work smarter, not harder.

Part 2: AI and the Future of jobs

4. The Jobs AI Will Create and Replace

A Déjà vu. The Industrial Revolution, which began in the late 18th and early 19th centuries, was a time of significant technological and social change. It marked the transition from hand-crafted goods and agrarian economies to industrialized production using machines. While machines replaced many traditional jobs, they also created entirely new industries and employment opportunities, reshaping the workforce and the economy.

AI is poised to replace jobs much like machines did during the Industrial Revolution by automating repetitive, routine, and labor-intensive tasks. Just as mechanized looms replaced skilled weavers and steam engines reduced the need for manual labor, AI-powered tools are automating tasks in several fields. Some industries are more at risk of disruption by AI and automation because they involve tasks that are repetitive, routine, or can easily be done by machines. Jobs in these industries are often centered around predictable processes, which makes them ideal for AI and automation to take over. Here are a few examples:

Manufacturing is one of the most affected industries because many tasks involve repetitive assembly line work. Robots powered by AI can work faster, more accurately, and without breaks, which makes them cost-effective for companies. For instance, car manufacturers use robotic arms to weld, paint, and assemble parts. While automation increases efficiency, it can reduce the need for human workers in roles that don't require creativity or problem-solving.

Transportation and Logistics. Transportation is being transformed by technologies like self-driving vehicles. Companies such as Tesla, Waymo, and Uber are developing autonomous cars and trucks, which could eventually replace drivers in the ride-hailing and freight industries. In logistics, warehouses are increasingly using AI-powered robots to pick, pack, and ship items, like the robots used in Amazon's fulfillment centers. These advancements reduce costs but threaten jobs for truck drivers, delivery personnel, and warehouse workers.

Retail and Customer Service. Retail jobs, especially those involving tasks like cashiering, are at risk due to AI. Automated checkout systems and cashier-less stores (like Amazon Go) are reducing the need for human cashiers. In customer service, chatbots and virtual assistants powered by AI are replacing customer service representatives by handling common inquiries, processing returns, or helping with orders online.

Data Entry and Administrative Roles. Jobs that involve routine data processing, entry, and scheduling are highly susceptible to automation. AI tools can process data much faster and more accurately than humans. For example, software like UiPath and Blue Prism automates tasks like inputting data into spreadsheets or generating reports. Similarly, AI tools like Calendly can handle scheduling without human intervention.

Banking and Finance. Many repetitive tasks in banking, such as loan processing, financial analysis, and fraud detection, are being automated. AI systems can evaluate creditworthiness, identify fraudulent transactions, and generate financial reports in seconds. This reduces the need for roles like bank tellers or entry-level analysts in areas where AI tools can perform the work efficiently.

Why These Industries Are Most at Risk? Industries most vulnerable to AI and automation are those where tasks are routine, predictable, and rule based. Machines and algorithms excel at repetitive work because they don't get tired, make fewer errors, and can process massive amounts of data quickly. While this increases productivity for businesses, it often reduces the demand for human workers in roles where creativity, emotional intelligence, or complex decision-making isn't required. That said, while AI and automation may replace some jobs, they also create new opportunities in areas like AI maintenance, programming, and more creative or strategic roles that machines cannot easily replicate. Adaptability and learning new skills will be key to thriving in this changing landscape.

Could AI create jobs? Going back to the example of the Industrial Revolution, which did not just eliminate jobs, but it also created new ones. As factories grew, they needed workers to operate the machines, maintain them, and oversee production processes. While these roles were often less skilled and lower-paying than traditional crafts, they provided employment to a growing population moving to cities in search of work. This shift from rural to urban living fueled the rise of industrial towns and cities.

New industries also emerged around the machines themselves. Engineers, machinists, and mechanics were needed to design, build, and repair the machinery. The growth of factories spurred demand for transportation infrastructure, leading to jobs building canals, railways, and steamships to move goods more efficiently. Additionally, industries like coal mining expanded to fuel the steam engines, creating jobs in resource extraction.

Similarly, AI is not only transforming industries but also creating new opportunities and jobs in areas that did not exist before. One key area is **data analysis**, where AI tools empower professionals to process and interpret massive amounts of information quickly and efficiently. Data analysts work with AI to uncover insights, trends, and predictions that drive decision-making in industries like healthcare, finance, and marketing. For instance, AI-powered analytics can help companies personalize customer experiences, optimize supply chains, or predict equipment failures in manufacturing, making data analysis a vital and growing field.

Another significant area is **AI system management and development**, which includes roles like AI trainers, system operators, and maintenance experts. AI trainers teach systems to recognize specific patterns, such as identifying images or processing human language. AI system managers ensure that these tools operate effectively, troubleshoot problems, and optimize performance. Additionally, new roles like **AI ethicists** focus on ensuring that AI is developed and deployed responsibly, addressing issues like bias, privacy, and transparency. These jobs, alongside positions in AI engineering and machine learning, represent exciting opportunities for individuals to shape the future of technology while driving innovation across multiple sectors.

An important message to the junior folks, heading into the job market. Adaptability is crucial as AI begins to take over certain jobs, reshaping industries, and the nature of work. Workers who can embrace change and pivot their careers to align with emerging opportunities will be better equipped to thrive in this evolving landscape. For instance, while AI might automate routine tasks in roles like data entry or customer service, it creates demand for skills in areas like data analysis, AI maintenance, and ethical oversight. The ability to learn modern technologies, develop transferable skills, and approach change with a growth mindset allows individuals to transition into these new roles. Moreover, adaptability fosters resilience, helping workers remain relevant by continually updating their knowledge and aligning their careers with the innovations AI brings. This mindset ensures that technological progress becomes an opportunity rather than a threat.

5. Skills of the Future

While AI excels at processing data, automating repetitive tasks, and analyzing patterns, there are key soft skills it cannot replicate (at least until now) – skills rooted in uniquely human traits like creativity, critical thinking, and emotional intelligence. These abilities remain essential in the workplace, as they allow humans to complement AI systems and tackle challenges that machines cannot address on their own.

Creativity is one of the most valuable soft skills that AI cannot fully replace, *yet*. While AI can generate ideas, write text, or create visuals based on existing data, it lacks the ability to think outside the box or imagine entirely new concepts. True creativity involves intuition, personal experience, and the ability to connect seemingly unrelated ideas in innovative ways. This is why roles in design, storytelling, product innovation, and artistic expression remain distinctively human. For example, while AI might suggest trends for a marketing campaign, the creative vision that resonates emotionally with an audience still comes from people.

Critical thinking is another area where humans outshine AI. AI can analyze data and offer recommendations, but it cannot evaluate those recommendations in the broader context of ethics, cultural nuances, or long-term impact. Critical thinking involves questioning assumptions, assessing the credibility of information, and making informed decisions based on complex, sometimes contradictory factors. In roles like leadership, strategy, or policymaking, humans use critical thinking to weigh risks, interpret subtleties, and navigate uncertainty in ways that machines cannot.

Emotional intelligence – the ability to understand and manage emotions, empathize with others, and build relationships – is a vital skill that AI cannot fully replicate. AI lacks genuine emotional understanding, which is critical for roles involving negotiation, conflict resolution, leadership, and caregiving. For example, in customer service or team management, a human's ability to read body language, detect subtle emotional cues, and respond with empathy makes all the difference in creating meaningful connections and resolving issues effectively. While chatbots can handle basic queries, human empathy and emotional intelligence are irreplaceable when navigating complex or sensitive interactions. Together, these soft skills enable humans to work alongside AI systems in ways that amplify both productivity and creativity. As AI continues to evolve, it will be those who can combine technical competence with uniquely human qualities who will thrive in the workforce, shaping a future where technology and humanity work hand in hand.

Given the advancement in AI, could it at some point gather human-like soft skills? For AI to fully replace humans in roles requiring creativity and soft skills, it would need to achieve artificial general intelligence (AGI) – a state where it could think, reason, and understand at a human level. This would require not just processing vast amounts of data but also developing self-awareness, intuition, and the ability to independently create meaning and values. While some researchers believe AGI could be possible in the *not very* distant future, it remains a theoretical concept for now, and the moral and ethical implications of such a development are profound.

In summary, while AI may continue to augment human capabilities, completely replacing humans in roles requiring creativity and emotional intelligence is unlikely in the near term. Instead, a collaborative model where AI enhances human potential while people provide uniquely human qualities seems to be the most probable path forward, as discussed in the following section.

Skills to learn. Hard skills like coding, data literacy, and understanding AI tools are in high demand as technology reshapes industries worldwide. **Coding**, often called the "language of the future," is a foundational skill for many tech careers, allowing people to build websites, apps, and even robots. Fun fact: the first programmer wasn't a computer scientist but a mathematician – **Ada Lovelace**, who wrote the first algorithm in the 1800s for Charles Babbage's early mechanical computer! Today, learning coding languages like Python, JavaScript, or C++ opens doors to fields like software development, game design, and artificial intelligence.

Data literacy is another crucial skill, as data has become the "new oil" of the digital age. Companies rely on people who can collect, analyze, and interpret data to make informed decisions. Did you know that every day, over **2.5 quintillion bytes** of data are created? That's enough to fill about 10 million Blu-ray discs! Tools like Excel, SQL, and Tableau help professionals turn raw data into visual insights, making data-driven strategies more accessible. Whether it's predicting customer preferences or optimizing supply chains, data literacy empowers individuals to harness this wealth of information.

Lastly, **understanding AI tools** is essential as artificial intelligence becomes integral to industries like healthcare, finance, and marketing. AI tools, like TensorFlow and Scikit-learn, enable people to build intelligent systems that can recognize patterns, make predictions, or even have conversations. AI is even being used to compose music, with some systems capable of writing entire symphonies inspired by classical composers! Developing expertise in AI tools equips individuals to create innovative solutions, from personal assistants to self-driving cars, making it one of the most exciting and versatile hard skills to learn today.

If you are looking for detailed advice for acquiring these skills through online platforms and local programs, the next few pages are for you. Otherwise, you can skip the following.

Acquiring in-demand skills like coding, data literacy, and understanding AI tools is more accessible than ever, thanks to the wealth of online platforms and local programs. Here's practical advice to help you get started:

Coding

- **Online Platforms:** Websites like Codecademy, freeCodeCamp, and Udemy offer beginner-friendly courses in languages like Python, JavaScript, and HTML. These platforms provide interactive exercises, projects, and certifications to help you build your skills step-by-step.

- **Practice Projects:** Create small, practical projects to solidify your learning, like building a personal website or developing a simple app. Platforms like GitHub allow you to share your work and collaborate with others.

- **Local Resources:** Many cities have coding bootcamps, like General Assembly or Flatiron School, offering immersive, hands-on training in software development. Community colleges also frequently offer affordable coding courses.

Data Literacy

- **Beginner Courses:** Platforms like Coursera and edX host courses on data analysis and visualization from top universities, often available for free with a certificate option. Look for courses covering Excel, SQL, or Tableau.

- **Specialized Tools:** Practice using real-world data sets available on Kaggle, where you can participate in competitions to apply your skills. Websites like DataCamp and LinkedIn Learning also provide interactive tutorials tailored to various levels.

- **Local Workshops:** Check for local meetups or workshops run by data-focused organizations. Many public libraries or community centers offer free or low-cost classes on data analysis and visualization.

Understanding AI Tools

- **Foundational Knowledge:** Start with introductory courses like Andrew Ng's "Machine Learning" on Coursera, which is widely regarded as a beginner-friendly guide to AI and machine learning principles.

- **Hands-On Practice:** Platforms like Google Colab and Kaggle offer free environments to experiment with AI tools like TensorFlow, PyTorch, or Scikit-learn using real data sets.

- **Community Engagement:** Join AI-focused communities on Meetup or forums like Reddit and Discord. These groups often share free resources, host events, and provide mentorship opportunities.

- **Local Programs:** Universities and colleges often run short AI and machine learning workshops or certificate programs for working professionals, offering access to both education and networking.

General Tips for Success

- **Set Clear Goals:** Focus on one skill at a time, and break your learning into manageable milestones.

- **Stay Consistent:** Dedicate a specific amount of time each day or week to learning and practicing.

- **Leverage Free Resources:** Many platforms offer free trials or courses, so you can test multiple tools before committing financially.

- **Join a community:** Learning with peers or mentors can keep you motivated and provide valuable feedback.

By combining these resources and staying consistent, you can build the skills needed to thrive in the tech-driven future!

6. **Collaboration with AI**

AI is increasingly proving to be a collaborator rather than a competitor, enhancing human capabilities rather than replacing them. By automating repetitive and time-consuming tasks, AI allows people to focus on more creative, strategic, and emotionally complex aspects of their work. This collaboration not only boosts productivity but also helps individuals unlock new opportunities to innovate and grow in their fields.

One way AI acts as a collaborator is by serving as a powerful assistant. For instance, in creative fields, AI tools like Adobe Sensei can suggest design improvements or automate tedious editing tasks, allowing designers to spend more time on the artistic aspects of their work. Similarly, AI-powered writing assistants like Grammarly or ChatGPT can help authors refine their language, generate ideas, or outline entire projects. Fun fact: AI has even co-authored books and scripts, showcasing its potential to contribute creatively alongside human partners.

AI is also revolutionizing data-heavy industries by acting as a "co-pilot" for professionals. Tools like Tableau or Power BI analyze massive datasets, presenting insights that help users make informed decisions faster. In healthcare, for example, AI-powered diagnostic tools assist doctors by identifying patterns in medical images that might be missed by the human eye. However, the final diagnosis and treatment decisions remain firmly in the hands of medical professionals. This dynamic exemplifies how AI supports human expertise rather than replacing it.

A cool example of AI collaboration is its use in music and art. AI systems like OpenAI's MuseNet can compose original pieces of music in various styles, often working with human composers who refine and personalize the final product. AI-powered tools like DALL·E and MidJourney allow artists to explore new creative territories by generating visual concepts they can develop further. These tools don't replace the artist's vision – they amplify it, offering fresh perspectives and ideas.

The key to making AI a collaborator rather than a competitor lies in leveraging its strengths – speed, efficiency, and data processing – while pairing them with uniquely human skills like creativity, emotional intelligence, and critical thinking. When humans and AI work together, the result is often greater than the sum of its parts. As AI continues to evolve, its role as a collaborator will empower people to achieve more, faster, and with greater precision, while leaving space for the distinctly human aspects of ingenuity and innovation.

Part 3: AI in Education and Learning

7. AI-Powered Learning Tools

AI is transforming education and learning by personalizing experiences, making education more accessible, and streamlining administrative tasks. AI-driven platforms like Duolingo and Khan Academy adapt to individual learning styles, helping students progress at their own pace and improving comprehension. It also expands access to quality education by offering online courses and AI-powered tutoring, breaking down geographical and financial barriers. For educators, AI automates tasks like grading and tracking student performance, allowing more time for teaching and mentorship. This blend of personalization, efficiency, and accessibility highlights AI's potential to revolutionize the way we learn and teach.

Popular AI-driven platforms like **Duolingo** and **Khan Academy** are revolutionizing education by leveraging artificial intelligence to create personalized and effective learning experiences.

- **Duolingo**: This language-learning app uses AI to tailor lessons to each user's skill level and progress. For example, its adaptive algorithms analyze how well you're mastering vocabulary and grammar, adjusting future lessons to focus on areas where you need improvement. Duolingo's AI also employs gamification techniques – like earning points and streaks – to keep learners engaged. Fun fact: Duolingo's AI can even predict when you're likely to forget a word and remind you to practice it before it fades from memory!

- **Khan Academy**: This platform provides free educational content on subjects like math, science, and history. Its AI-driven tools, such as Khanmigo, offer personalized learning paths based on a student's strengths and weaknesses. For instance, in math lessons, the system identifies where a student struggles (e.g., fractions or algebra) and suggests targeted practice exercises. AI also powers Khan Academy's virtual tutors, providing real-time feedback and hints to help students understand complex concepts.

Both platforms showcase how AI can make education more accessible, engaging, and tailored to individual needs, helping millions of learners worldwide achieve their goals. Here are some practical tips for maximizing the benefits of AI tools in personal education:

Identify Your Learning Goals. Clearly define what you want to achieve, whether it's mastering a new language, improving math skills, or learning to code. Knowing your goals will help you choose the most suitable AI tools and features.

Choose the Right Platform. Research AI-driven platforms tailored to your needs. For instance, use **Duolingo** for language learning, **Khan Academy** for academic subjects, or **DataCamp** for data science and coding. Many platforms offer free trials, so explore before committing.

Take Advantage of Personalization. Allow the AI tool to assess your current skill level. These platforms often use adaptive learning to focus on your weaknesses, making your study time more efficient. Be consistent in using the tool so it can track your progress and adjust accordingly.

Set a Schedule and Stick to It. Consistency is key. Use AI tools to set reminders, create a study schedule, and track your learning streaks. Many platforms gamify the process with badges or streak counters to keep you motivated.

Engage with Supplemental Features. Many AI tools offer additional features like quizzes, virtual tutors, or peer discussions. For example, platforms like **Khan Academy** and **Coursera** provide practice exercises and forums where you can deepen your understanding by interacting with other learners.

Monitor Your Progress. Regularly review the progress reports provided by the AI tool to see where you're excelling and what needs improvement. Use this information to adjust your study approach or revisit challenging topics.

Combine AI with Other Resources. Don't rely solely on AI tools. Use them alongside traditional learning methods like reading books, attending workshops, or participating in group discussions for a well-rounded learning experience.

Be Proactive in Asking for Help. Many AI platforms provide virtual tutors or forums where you can ask questions. If you're stuck, use these resources to clarify doubts rather than moving forward with gaps in understanding.

Protect Your Data and Privacy. Be mindful of the data you share with these tools. Use strong passwords and only share necessary information to protect your privacy.

Reflect and Adapt. Periodically evaluate whether the AI tool is helping you meet your goals. If not, consider switching to a different platform or adjusting your approach.

By incorporating these tips, you can effectively use AI tools to enhance your learning experience, making education more engaging, personalized, and productive.

8. Preparing the Next Generation.

Schools are increasingly incorporating AI into their curricula to prepare students for a future where technology plays a vital role. From teaching foundational coding skills to fostering innovation through robotics clubs, schools are equipping students with the tools they need to understand and work with artificial intelligence.

Coding Lessons and AI Concepts. Many schools now introduce coding lessons as early as elementary school, using platforms like Scratch, Code.org, and Tynker to teach the basics in a fun and interactive way. As students advance, they explore programming languages like Python and JavaScript, which are foundational for AI development. Some schools go further by offering courses specifically focused on AI concepts, such as machine learning, neural networks, and data science. For example, students might use AI tools to analyze real-world data or create simple AI models that recognize patterns or predict outcomes.

Robotics Clubs. Robotics clubs provide hands-on opportunities for students to apply AI and coding in creative ways. Using kits like LEGO Mindstorms or Arduino, students design and program robots to perform tasks such as navigating mazes or responding to voice commands. These projects teach problem-solving, teamwork, and technical skills, all while making AI concepts accessible and engaging. Some schools participate in competitions like FIRST Robotics or VEX Robotics, where students design AI-driven robots to tackle specific challenges, sparking innovation and friendly rivalry.

AI-Driven Tools in Classrooms. Schools are also using AI-powered educational tools to enhance learning across subjects. For example, platforms like Khan Academy and Quizlet adapt to individual student progress, offering personalized lessons and practice exercises. Some schools use AI to support teachers by automating grading or identifying students who need extra help through learning analytics.

Ethical and Societal Discussions. In addition to technical skills, schools are fostering critical thinking by engaging students in discussions about the ethical implications of AI. Topics like data privacy, bias in AI, and the societal impact of automation are integrated into the curriculum, encouraging students to think about how technology influences the world around them.

By integrating AI through coding lessons, robotics clubs, and advanced learning tools, schools are not only teaching technical skills but also inspiring curiosity and preparing students to be leaders in an AI-driven future.

Parents should be on board rather than fearing AI. To encourage tech literacy in children, parents can start by introducing age-appropriate coding and STEM activities through interactive platforms like **Scratch**, **Code.org**, or **Tynker**, which make learning fun and engaging. Encouraging exploration by providing access to robotics kits or science projects that involve technology, such as building simple circuits or programming a robot. Fostering curiosity by discussing how technology impacts everyday life, from smartphones to smart homes, and encourage children to ask questions about how things work. Lastly, setting a positive example by learning alongside your children and emphasizing the importance of balancing screen time with hands-on, creative activities.

There is no escape from AI in education. There is a heated debate among educators about the use of AI in education and learning, and the ethical side of this new technology. While some educators choose completely to ban the use of AI in their classes, many other educators understand that there is no way we can avoid the use of AI in the classroom or in education in general. Therefore, the best way forward is to train the students in the best ways of using this technology and encourage ethical usage of it.

Teaching ethical considerations around AI is crucial as this technology becomes increasingly integrated into society. AI systems can greatly impact decision-making processes, from hiring practices to loan approvals and even law enforcement. Without ethical oversight, these systems can unintentionally perpetuate biases, invade privacy, or make decisions that lack transparency. By educating future generations about these challenges, we empower them to create and use AI responsibly, ensuring it benefits everyone fairly and equitably.

Discussing ethics in AI also fosters critical thinking about technology's societal implications. Students learn to question how data is collected and used, whether algorithms treat all groups fairly, and how AI can impact jobs and human interactions. These lessons prepare them to navigate and shape a future where technology is deeply entwined with daily life. Moreover, understanding AI ethics helps individuals advocate for regulations and policies that prioritize fairness, accountability, and privacy, ensuring that AI serves as a tool for progress rather than a source of harm. Teaching ethical considerations today ensures that tomorrow's innovators and decision-makers approach AI with responsibility and humanity.

9. Upskilling for Adults

The growing trend of adult learners using platforms like **Coursera**, **Udemy**, and **LinkedIn Learning** reflects the increasing demand for flexible, accessible education in today's fast-changing job market. These platforms cater to professionals seeking to enhance their skills, shift careers, or stay competitive by offering a wide variety of courses in fields like programming, data science, business, and creative arts. Courses are often self-paced, allowing learners to balance their studies with work or personal commitments. For example, a working parent can learn Python or project management in the evenings, leveraging content from industry leaders or top universities without needing to enroll in a traditional degree program.

One of the key drivers behind this trend is the rapid pace of technological advancement. With industries evolving quickly, professionals need to continuously upskill to remain relevant. Platforms like Coursera and LinkedIn Learning partner with organizations like Google, IBM, and Microsoft to provide certifications in high-demand areas such as AI, cloud computing, and digital marketing. These credentials are often recognized by employers, making them valuable for career progression. Additionally, many courses are interactive, offering hands-on projects, quizzes, and peer feedback, ensuring practical, real-world learning. This trend highlights how online education is empowering adults to adapt, grow, and thrive in an ever-changing professional landscape.

If you are interested in improving your AI or computing skills, here is a step-by-step guide to identifying skill gaps and addressing them with AI resources:

Step 1: Evaluate Your Current Skills

- **Assess Your Role and Industry Requirements**: Make a list of the skills needed in your current job or the career you aspire to. Check job descriptions or talk to colleagues to understand what's expected.
- **Reflect on Strengths and Weaknesses**: Think about tasks you find challenging or areas where you rely heavily on others. For example, are you struggling with data analysis or project management?
- **Use AI Tools for Self-Assessment**: Platforms like LinkedIn's Skills Assessment quizzes or AI-driven career guidance tools like MyPath can help pinpoint areas where you might lack proficiency.

Step 2: Research Industry Trends

- **Identify Emerging Skills**: Look for trends in your industry to find skills that are becoming essential, such as knowledge of AI tools, programming, or digital marketing.
- **Use AI Insights**: Tools like Burning Glass or LinkedIn Learning's Skills Insights analyze market trends and highlight in-demand skills for your profession.

Step 3: Prioritize Skill Gaps

- **Rank Skills by Relevance**: Focus on skills that align with your career goals and are most impactful in your field. For example, if your role involves working with data, prioritize data literacy or visualization.
- **Set Clear Goals**: Decide which skill gaps you want to address first, and set realistic milestones (e.g., learn basic Python in two months).

Step 4: Choose AI-Powered Learning Platforms

- **Explore Online Resources**: Use platforms like Coursera, Udemy, or LinkedIn Learning for structured courses. For example, Coursera offers certificates in machine learning and business analytics from top universities.
- **Leverage AI Tutoring Tools**: Tools like Khan Academy or DataCamp adapt to your learning pace, focusing on areas where you need improvement.
- **Practice with Real-World Applications**: Platforms like Kaggle allow you to work on datasets to enhance practical skills.

Step 5: Create a Learning Schedule

- **Allocate Time for Learning**: Dedicate specific hours each week to learning. Use AI-driven productivity tools like Notion or Todoist to organize your schedule and set reminders.
- **Start Small**: Begin with foundational courses and gradually move to advanced topics to avoid overwhelm.

Step 6: Apply Your Learning

- **Work on Projects**: Use your new skills in real-world or simulated projects. For example, build a simple AI model or create dashboards using data visualization tools.
- **Join Communities**: Participate in forums like Stack Overflow, LinkedIn groups, or Discord communities where you can collaborate with peers and seek feedback.

Step 7: Track Progress

- **Use AI Feedback**: Many platforms provide progress reports and insights into your strengths and areas that need more practice.
- **Self-Evaluate**: Regularly test your skills through quizzes, certifications, or by solving practical challenges.

Step 8: Stay Updated

- **Continuous Learning**: Technology evolves rapidly, so keep up with updates and trends by subscribing to newsletters, attending webinars, or exploring advanced courses.
- **Experiment with New AI Tools**: Familiarize yourself with emerging technologies relevant to your field to maintain a competitive edge.

By following these steps and leveraging AI-powered resources, you can systematically identify and address your skill gaps, positioning yourself for growth in a rapidly evolving job market. *Note: There are several AI related courses from top Universities and research institutions offered free of charge – keep an eye out.*

Part 4: AI in Scientific Research

10. How is AI revolutionizing scientific research?

This topic is of particular interest for me given that I deal with it on a day-to-day basis. For example In my field (astrophysics), coding, Machine Learning, deep learning, neural networks, and AI are becoming an integral part of our work. So how is AI revolutionizing Research?

AI is revolutionizing scientific research by enabling scientists to process massive datasets, identify patterns, and make predictions that were previously impossible. By automating routine tasks and offering unprecedented insights, AI accelerates discoveries and opens new frontiers in various fields. Here's a brief summary of how AI is making strides in specific scientific domains:

Astronomy. AI is helping astronomers analyze vast amounts of data generated by ground- and space-based survey missions, enabling them to detect and study celestial objects more efficiently. For example, AI algorithms have been used to identify new exoplanets by analyzing light curves from stars, as seen in the *Kepler* Space Telescope data. These algorithms detect subtle dips in brightness caused by planets passing in front of stars. AI tools like Google's DeepMind are assisting in mapping cosmic structures and identifying gravitational waves, providing insights into the origins and evolution of the universe. Surveys like the

Vera Rubin Observatory, an 8.4-m telescope under construction in Chile, designed to scan a large part of the sky on nightly basis to discover faint transient astronomical phenomena and study dark matter and dark energy, will be relying heavily on AI in its operation and data analysis. It will process images of the entire visible sky every **three nights**, collecting data on billions of celestial objects, including stars, galaxies, and asteroids. The survey is expected to generate a staggering amount of data – **approximately 20 terabytes per night** (a terabyte is 1000 gigabytes; your smartphone typically has between 64 and 256 gigabytes of storage). This means that the survey will generate about **60 petabytes** of raw data over the course of its 10 years. To put this into perspective; the observatory will capture **10 million gigabytes** of data annually, which is roughly equivalent to the storage capacity of 20,000 standard laptops (each with 500 GB storage). You have guessed it right – *it won't be possible for scientists to process this massive amount of data without the help of the machine.*

The Vera Rubin Observatory's unprecedented data output highlights the critical role of AI and advanced computing in astronomy. AI will help process, analyze, and prioritize the data, enabling scientists to detect rare and transient phenomena, such as supernovae, near-Earth asteroids, and gravitational lensing events, in near real-time. This massive undertaking will provide unparalleled insights into the universe's structure, evolution, and mysteries like dark matter and dark energy.

Physics. In physics, AI aids in modeling complex systems, discovering new materials, and solving intricate equations. AI was instrumental in detecting the Higgs boson (aka the god's particle) by analyzing data from the Large Hadron Collider, sifting through enormous datasets to find rare particle interactions. AI Is also being used in quantum physics to optimize quantum circuits and identify patterns in quantum states, which could lead to advancements in quantum computing.

Biology. AI accelerates research in genomics, protein folding, and ecosystem modeling by handling large biological datasets. DeepMind's AlphaFold solved the decades-old challenge of protein structure prediction, a breakthrough that aids drug discovery and understanding diseases. In ecological studies, AI models analyze satellite data to monitor deforestation, track wildlife populations, and predict the impact of climate change on ecosystems.

Medicine. AI is transforming medicine by improving diagnostics, drug discovery, and personalized treatments. For example, AI-powered diagnostic tools like those used for detecting breast cancer or diabetic retinopathy analyze medical images with accuracy comparable to, or better than, human experts. AI is also accelerating drug discovery, as seen during the COVID-19 pandemic, where AI models identified potential therapeutic compounds in record time. For example, AI from BenevolentAI helped identify baricitinib as a potential treatment for COVID-19 patients.

Chemistry. AI in chemistry is revolutionizing material discovery, reaction optimization, and molecular modeling: AI algorithms have designed novel materials, such as advanced batteries and superconductors, by predicting properties of chemical compounds. Moreover, researchers are using AI to predict chemical reaction outcomes, saving time and resources in drug development and industrial applications.

As AI continues to evolve, it will become an even more integral part of scientific research, helping us solve some of the most complex challenges across disciplines.

Part 5: Ethical Considerations and Challenges

11. The Double-Edged Sword of AI

Artificial intelligence (AI) is often described as a transformative technology with the potential to revolutionize industries, enhance productivity, and fuel innovation. On the positive side, AI excels at efficiency, handling tasks faster and more accurately than humans. For example, in manufacturing, AI-powered robots assemble products with precision, reducing waste and production costs. In healthcare, AI systems analyze medical images and identify diseases like cancer with remarkable accuracy, enabling earlier diagnoses and better patient outcomes. Moreover, AI drives innovation by uncovering patterns and opportunities that were previously invisible, such as predicting climate trends or developing personalized medicines. These benefits allow organizations to achieve breakthroughs and improve the quality of life for millions of people.

However, AI is not without its challenges, and its transformative power also comes with risks. One major concern is job displacement. As AI automates routine and repetitive tasks, roles in industries like manufacturing, retail, and data entry are being eliminated. This can create economic insecurity for workers who may not have the skills to transition into emerging roles. While new jobs are created by AI, such as AI system managers or data scientists, they often require specialized training, which can widen the skills gap and exacerbate inequality.

Another significant risk of AI lies in its potential for bias and ethical issues. AI systems learn from data, and if that data reflects existing societal biases, the AI can perpetuate or even amplify them. For instance, biased AI algorithms in hiring systems or loan approvals have led to unfair treatment of certain groups. Additionally, AI's use in surveillance and decision-making raises privacy concerns and ethical dilemmas, such as whether it is acceptable to use AI in law enforcement or military applications. These risks highlight the need for transparent and accountable AI development practices.

The double-edged nature of AI underscores the importance of balancing its benefits with its challenges. By implementing responsible AI practices, investing in reskilling programs, and addressing ethical concerns, society can harness AI's potential while mitigating its risks. This approach ensures that AI serves as a tool for progress, rather than a source of harm or division.

AI is not perfect; it can fail sometimes. While artificial intelligence holds great promise, real-world examples of AI failures illustrate its significant risks and limitations. One notable instance is the issue of biased hiring algorithms. In 2018, a hiring tool developed by Amazon was revealed to have discriminatory tendencies against women. The AI, trained on historical hiring data from the company, learned to favor male candidates because the data reflected past biases where more men were hired for technical roles. As a result, the system penalized resumes that included terms like "women's chess club captain" or those from women-only colleges. This case underscores how AI can inherit and amplify societal biases if the training data is not properly vetted for fairness.

Flawed facial recognition systems present another stark example of AI's shortcomings. Research has repeatedly shown that facial recognition technologies, such as those from IBM and Microsoft, have higher error rates when identifying individuals with darker skin tones or women compared to lighter-skinned males. In one study by MIT Media Lab, commercial AI systems misidentified Black women up to 34% of the time, while error rates for white men were under 1%. These disparities have serious implications when facial recognition is used in high-stakes areas like law enforcement. In one widely publicized case, Robert Williams, a Black man, was wrongfully arrested in Detroit in 2020 due to a facial recognition error, highlighting how flawed AI systems can lead to life-altering consequences.

AI failures are not limited to biases; they can also arise from poor oversight or unintended consequences. For instance, an AI-powered content moderation system used by social media platforms incorrectly flagged and removed posts that were harmless or educational, such as posts about historical atrocities or health awareness. This highlights how AI's lack of context and nuance can result in overreach, restricting freedom of expression or access to important information.

These examples demonstrate the double-edged nature of AI, where its potential for efficiency and innovation is counterbalanced by the risks of bias, inaccuracy, and unintended harm. They highlight the urgent need for ethical guidelines, rigorous testing, and diverse data sets in AI development to prevent such failures. By addressing these challenges proactively, we can strive for AI systems that are not only powerful but also equitable and trustworthy.

Adopting a balanced view of AI's capabilities and limitations is essential for understanding its role in shaping our future. AI has the power to revolutionize industries, improve lives, and solve complex problems with incredible efficiency. From diagnosing diseases early to optimizing global supply chains, its benefits are undeniable. However, AI is not a magic solution, nor is it infallible. It relies on the quality of its data and programming, and its effectiveness is limited by the scope of its design. Recognizing these strengths and weaknesses allows us to appreciate AI's potential while remaining mindful of its challenges.

By maintaining a balanced perspective, we can make informed decisions about how to integrate AI into our lives and society responsibly. This means celebrating its achievements while also questioning its ethical implications, addressing its biases, and ensuring accountability in its development. Rather than viewing AI as an all-powerful force or a threat to humanity, we should approach it as a tool—one that, when used thoughtfully and with care, can enhance our world without compromising our values. With a balanced mindset, we can harness AI's capabilities to their fullest while actively mitigating its risks.

12. Data Privacy and Security

AI relies heavily on personal data to function effectively, as this data enables it to learn, adapt, and provide personalized experiences. For example, AI systems in social media platforms use personal data, such as likes, shares, and browsing habits, to curate content tailored to individual preferences. Similarly, virtual assistants like Siri and Alexa analyze voice commands and user behavior to offer relevant responses and recommendations. Even AI in healthcare leverages patient data to predict diagnoses and recommend treatments. By processing vast amounts of personal information, AI can deliver highly efficient and personalized services.

However, the use of personal data by AI comes with significant risks. One major concern is **data privacy**. AI systems often collect more information than users realize, ranging from location data to online activity, which can be misused if not properly secured. For instance, a data breach can expose sensitive information, leading to identity theft or financial fraud. Additionally, users may have little control over how their data is collected, stored, or shared, raising ethical questions about consent and transparency.

Another risk is **bias and discrimination**. If the data used to train AI systems reflects societal biases or inequalities, the AI can perpetuate and even amplify those biases. For example, facial recognition systems trained on unrepresentative datasets have shown higher error rates for certain demographics, leading to unfair outcomes in areas like law enforcement or hiring. These biases are often difficult to detect, making them harder to address and mitigate.

Lastly, the concentration of personal data in the hands of a few powerful companies raises concerns about surveillance and loss of autonomy. AI systems could be used for intrusive monitoring, such as tracking individuals' online behavior to influence their decisions, from targeted advertising to political campaigns. This level of data collection can erode trust and create a chilling effect on free expression.

To mitigate these risks, robust data protection measures, transparency in AI systems, and ethical guidelines are essential. Users must also be educated about how their data is being used and given tools to control their information. By addressing these challenges, we can ensure that AI serves as a force for good while respecting individual privacy and rights. In Part 1 I have provided several actionable steps for protecting information, such using strong passwords and limiting data sharing. Below I highlight emerging tools for managing digital privacy:

Emerging tools for managing digital privacy are empowering individuals to regain control over their personal information in the age of AI and data-driven technology. **Privacy-focused browsers** like **Brave** and **DuckDuckGo** are gaining popularity by blocking trackers, limiting cookies, and preventing websites from collecting unnecessary user data. These tools prioritize anonymity and ensure that your browsing activity isn't monitored or sold to advertisers. Similarly, **virtual private networks (VPNs)** like **NordVPN** and **ExpressVPN** encrypt your internet connection, masking your location and making it harder for third parties to track your online activity. These tools are especially useful for safeguarding privacy when using public Wi-Fi networks.

Beyond browsers and VPNs, tools like **data-deletion services** and **personal data management platforms** are becoming more common. Services such as **Jumbo Privacy** and **DeleteMe** help users identify and remove personal information from data brokers and platforms where it may be stored. Additionally, **password managers** like **LastPass** and **Dashlane** enhance privacy by securely generating and storing strong, unique passwords, reducing the risk of breaches caused by weak or reused credentials. Emerging AI-powered privacy assistants are also helping users monitor and manage their digital footprints, providing real-time alerts about potential data exposures and suggesting actionable steps to enhance security. These tools make it easier for individuals to navigate the digital world while protecting their privacy.

13. AI and Society: The Bigger Picture

The societal implications of AI extend far beyond its technical applications, shaping how we live, interact, and make decisions. One significant concern is the role of AI in **surveillance**. Governments and corporations increasingly use AI-powered systems, such as facial recognition and behavior analysis, to monitor public spaces and individuals. While these tools can enhance security, they also raise serious privacy concerns. In authoritarian regimes, AI surveillance has been used to suppress dissent and track political opponents, eroding civil liberties. Even in democratic societies, the widespread adoption of surveillance technology can lead to overreach and a loss of anonymity, fostering a culture of constant monitoring.

Another critical issue is **misinformation**. AI-powered tools, such as deepfake technology and automated content generators, make it easier to create and distribute false or misleading information at scale. Deepfake videos can depict individuals saying or doing things they never did, undermining trust in media and public figures. Similarly, AI algorithms that prioritize engagement can unintentionally amplify misinformation on social media platforms, as controversial or sensational content often generates more clicks and shares. This poses significant risks to democratic processes, as misinformation can influence public opinion and elections.

Ethical decision-making in AI is another area with profound societal implications. AI systems are increasingly used in areas like hiring, loan approvals, law enforcement, and healthcare – domains where decisions can significantly impact people's lives. However, these systems often lack transparency and accountability, making it difficult to understand how decisions are made or challenge unfair outcomes. For example, biased algorithms have led to discriminatory practices in hiring or policing, perpetuating inequalities. The question of who is responsible for AI's decisions – developers, users, or the organizations deploying the technology – remains an ongoing ethical debate.

Addressing these societal challenges requires collaboration between governments, tech companies, and civil society. Regulations and policies must ensure that AI is developed and deployed responsibly, prioritizing transparency, accountability, and fairness. Public awareness and education about AI's societal implications are equally important, empowering individuals to make informed decisions and advocate for ethical practices. By recognizing both the benefits and risks of AI, we can work toward a future where technology serves humanity without compromising fundamental rights and values.

The Role of Governments and Corporations in Ensuring AI's Ethical Use. Governments and corporations play a crucial role in ensuring that AI is developed and used ethically, balancing innovation with the protection of human rights, fairness, and accountability. Their actions set the tone for how AI shapes society, influencing its benefits and mitigating its risks.

- **Governments: Setting the Legal and Ethical Framework**

Governments are responsible for establishing regulations and policies to ensure AI is used ethically and transparently. By creating standards for data privacy, algorithmic transparency, and accountability, governments can prevent misuse and ensure that AI systems are aligned with societal values. For example, the **European Union's General Data Protection Regulation (GDPR)** includes provisions that grant individuals the right to know when AI is used to make decisions about them and to contest automated decisions. Similarly, proposed legislation like the **EU AI Act** aims to classify AI applications by risk and enforce stricter oversight on high-risk systems, such as those used in law enforcement or hiring.

Governments also play a role in funding research into ethical AI practices and providing platforms for public dialogue on AI's implications. International cooperation is essential, as AI development often transcends national borders. Global bodies like the **United Nations** and **OECD** are working to create guidelines for the responsible use of AI, emphasizing principles like fairness, inclusivity, and accountability.

- **Corporations: Building Ethical AI by Design**

Corporations are at the forefront of AI development and deployment, making them critical stakeholders in ethical AI. Companies must adopt **ethical AI practices by design**, ensuring that fairness, privacy, and accountability are integrated into the development process. For example, many tech giants like Google, Microsoft, and IBM have established **AI ethics committees** to oversee projects and ensure that they align with ethical guidelines.

Transparency is a key responsibility for corporations. Companies should openly share how their AI systems work, including the data used for training and the decision-making processes behind their algorithms. Open-source initiatives, like OpenAI's commitment to sharing research, help foster accountability and collaboration across industries. Moreover, corporations can implement **bias detection tools** to identify and address discriminatory patterns in their algorithms, reducing the risk of harm to marginalized groups.

- **Joint Responsibility and Collaboration**

Governments and corporations must collaborate to ensure that ethical AI becomes a global standard. Public-private partnerships can fund research into addressing challenges like algorithmic bias, data security, and the environmental impact of AI. For instance, **AI4Good**, an initiative by the UN, brings together governments, businesses, and researchers to use AI to address global challenges like poverty, education, and climate change.

Ultimately, both governments and corporations must prioritize transparency, accountability, and public trust. While governments enforce regulations to protect individuals and society, corporations can lead by example, building AI systems that are not only innovative but also ethical and responsible. Together, their combined efforts can ensure that AI serves as a tool for progress while respecting fundamental human values.

Encouraging Conversations About AI Policy and Advocacy. As AI continues to shape our lives and societies, it is essential for everyone – not just technologists and policymakers – to engage in conversations about its impact. AI influences critical aspects of our world, from job markets and healthcare to privacy and freedom of expression. By participating in discussions about AI policy and advocacy, individuals can help ensure that these technologies are developed and used in ways that reflect shared values, promote fairness, and protect fundamental rights.

Engaging in AI policy discussions begins with staying informed about the key issues, such as algorithmic bias, data privacy, and the ethical implications of automation. Joining local or online forums, attending public talks, or following organizations like the **Partnership on AI** or the **Electronic Frontier Foundation (EFF)** can help individuals understand how AI policies are being shaped and contribute their perspectives. Advocacy doesn't have to be complex—it can start with raising awareness among peers or voicing opinions about AI-related decisions that affect local communities.

Individuals can also support initiatives aimed at ethical AI development by signing petitions, attending town hall meetings, or engaging with policymakers. For instance, advocating for transparent AI systems in public services, such as law enforcement or healthcare, ensures accountability and fairness. Encouraging diverse perspectives in AI policymaking helps address systemic biases and ensures that AI benefits society as a whole, not just a select few.

By participating in these conversations, readers contribute to shaping a future where AI is a tool for progress and equity. Advocacy and dialogue empower individuals to hold corporations and governments accountable, ensuring that AI technologies align with societal values and priorities. Together, collective voices can help steer AI's trajectory toward a more inclusive and ethical future.

Part 6: Thriving in an AI-Driven World

14. Adopting a Growth Mindset

Strategies for overcoming fear of AI and embracing change. As AI continues to transform industries and reshape daily life, it's natural to feel apprehensive about its impact. However, adopting a **growth mindset** – the belief that abilities and knowledge can be developed through effort and learning – can help individuals overcome fear of AI and embrace the opportunities it presents. By focusing on curiosity, adaptability, and lifelong learning, we can shift from fearing AI to leveraging its potential.

One strategy for overcoming fear is to **educate yourself about AI**. Much of the fear surrounding AI stems from misunderstanding its capabilities and limitations. AI is a powerful tool, but it is not infallible, sentient, or all-powerful. By learning how AI works and understanding its real-world applications, you can demystify the technology and recognize its value as a partner rather than a threat. Free or affordable resources, such as Coursera's "AI for Everyone" or Google's AI education tools, are excellent places to start.

Another key strategy is to **focus on skills that complement AI**. Rather than viewing AI as a competitor, recognize it as a collaborator that enhances human capabilities. By honing soft skills like creativity, critical thinking, and emotional intelligence – skills that AI cannot replicate – you position yourself to work alongside AI effectively. Additionally, embracing technical skills like basic coding or data literacy can help you understand and use AI tools with confidence, turning potential challenges into opportunities for growth.

Finally, adopt a mindset of **embracing change as a catalyst for growth**. Change can be uncomfortable, but it often leads to innovation and personal development. Instead of fearing disruption, approach it as an opportunity to explore new roles, acquire new skills, or solve problems in creative ways. Reflect on past instances when you adapted to change successfully and use those experiences to build resilience. Surround yourself with supportive communities or peers who share a similar mindset, as collaboration and shared learning can make navigating change less daunting.

By educating yourself, building complementary skills, and reframing change as an opportunity, you can transform fear into empowerment. A growth mindset allows you to embrace AI not as a threat, but as a tool to unlock new possibilities and shape a future where technology enhances, rather than replaces, human potential.

There are many inspiring stories of individuals who successfully adapted to new technologies. These stories are based on real life events, or are they? Regardless, it is all about the moral of the story:

- **The Librarian Who Became a Data Scientist**

Maria, a librarian in her mid-40s, faced a challenge when her role became increasingly digital, with fewer people visiting the library and more relying on online resources. Instead of resisting the shift, Maria embraced change by taking online courses in data analytics and machine learning through platforms like Coursera. She learned how to use tools like Python and Tableau to analyze library usage patterns and improve digital cataloging. Maria eventually transitioned into a new role as a data scientist for a nonprofit, using her analytical skills to optimize resource allocation for community projects. Her story highlights how learning new skills can open unexpected career paths.

- **The Taxi Driver Who Embraced Ride-Sharing Apps**

Ahmed, a taxi driver in a bustling city, initially saw ride-sharing platforms like Uber and Lyft as a threat to his livelihood. Rather than resist, he signed up as a driver for these services and leveraged their technology to maximize his earnings. By using the apps' data-driven features, such as heat maps that show areas with high demand, Ahmed learned to strategize his routes and reduce downtime. Over time, he became one of the platform's top-rated drivers in his area. Ahmed's willingness to adapt allowed him to not only sustain his income but also embrace technology to work smarter.

- **The Factory Worker Who Became a Robotics Technician**

Javier, a factory worker in his early 30s, saw his assembly line job at risk when the company announced plans to automate production. Rather than fear the automation, Javier enrolled in a local technical college's robotics program. He learned how to maintain and program the robots that were replacing manual labor on the assembly line. After completing his certification, Javier was promoted to a robotics technician role, where he ensures the smooth operation of the factory's automated systems. His proactive approach turned a potential job loss into a rewarding career advancement.

- **The Artist Who Explored AI-Powered Creativity**

Sophie, a freelance illustrator, faced growing competition in her field and was initially skeptical about AI tools like DALL·E and MidJourney. However, she decided to experiment with these platforms, using them to generate ideas and visual concepts that she could refine and personalize. By combining her artistic skills with AI-generated designs, Sophie was able to expand her client offerings and take on more ambitious projects. She now teaches workshops on integrating AI into creative processes, proving that technology can amplify, not replace, artistic vision.

- **The Teacher Who Became a Virtual Educator**

Liam, a high school teacher, found himself struggling during the pandemic when classrooms moved online. Instead of being overwhelmed by the shift to digital learning, he embraced platforms like Zoom, Google Classroom, and AI-powered teaching tools like Khan Academy. Liam used these technologies to create interactive virtual lessons, track student progress, and provide personalized feedback. His efforts not only kept his students engaged but also earned him recognition for innovative teaching. Today, Liam continues to blend AI tools with traditional teaching, setting a new standard for hybrid education.

These stories demonstrate how embracing technology with a growth mindset can lead to unexpected opportunities. By learning new skills, leveraging available tools, and remaining open to change, individuals can transform challenges into success stories in the digital age.

In the age of AI, continuous learning and self-improvement are not just beneficial – they are essential for staying relevant and thriving in an ever-evolving world. AI is transforming industries at an unprecedented pace, automating routine tasks and creating demand for new skills. To adapt to these changes, individuals must embrace lifelong learning as a core mindset. Unlike in the past, where a single degree or skillset might carry someone through an entire career, today's landscape requires constant growth and adaptability to meet the demands of a dynamic job market.

One of the key reasons continuous learning is so important is that AI is reshaping the nature of work. While it automates repetitive and predictable tasks, it simultaneously creates opportunities in areas requiring creativity, critical thinking, and emotional intelligence – skills that machines cannot replicate. By staying curious and open to learning, individuals can develop the technical skills needed to work alongside AI, such as data literacy or understanding how AI tools operate, as well as enhance uniquely human traits like leadership and problem-solving. This dual approach ensures they remain competitive and resilient, no matter how technology evolves.

Continuous self-improvement also empowers individuals to explore new career paths and passions that may emerge due to technological advancements. For example, fields like

AI ethics, virtual reality design, or green technology have grown rapidly in response to AI's integration into various industries. By investing time in upskilling through online courses, workshops, or mentorship programs, individuals can position themselves to take advantage of these opportunities and contribute meaningfully to the future of work.

Ultimately, the age of AI calls for a mindset shift – one that views learning as an ongoing process rather than a finite goal. By committing to continuous self-improvement, individuals not only future-proof their careers but also cultivate a sense of purpose, adaptability, and personal fulfillment. In a world where change is the only constant, the ability to learn and grow will remain the most valuable skill of all.

15. Leveraging AI for Personal Growth

AI offers a variety of tools that can significantly enhance productivity and support personal growth, making it easier to manage daily tasks, achieve goals, and unlock new opportunities. By integrating these tools into everyday routines, individuals can streamline their work, improve time management, and focus on high-value activities that contribute to their development.

Task Managers and Calendar Assistants. AI-powered task managers and calendar assistants help users organize their schedules, prioritize tasks, and stay on track with their goals. Tools like Microsoft To Do, Todoist, and Notion use AI to suggest deadlines, remind you of upcoming tasks, and even categorize to-do lists based on urgency. Calendar assistants, such as Google Calendar or Microsoft Outlook, use AI to schedule meetings, suggest optimal times based on availability, and send reminders. Advanced tools like Motion combine task management with scheduling, automatically arranging your day to maximize productivity and minimize conflicts.

Writing and Content Creation Tools. For those looking to improve communication and creativity, AI tools like Grammarly, Jasper, and ChatGPT can assist with drafting emails, drafting reports, or generating creative content. These tools not only help users save time but also ensure clarity, professionalism, and effectiveness in their writing. For content creators, AI platforms like Canva suggest design templates and layouts, while tools like Copy.ai generate marketing copy or social media posts tailored to specific audiences.

Learning and Skill Development Platforms. AI-powered learning platforms such as Duolingo, Khan Academy, and Coursera adapt to individual learning styles and paces. These tools use AI to identify areas where users struggle and tailor lessons, accordingly, helping them master new skills more efficiently. For coding or data science enthusiasts, platforms like DataCamp and Kaggle provide hands-on projects and challenges to apply what they've learned in real-world scenarios.

Financial Planning and Personal Management Tools. AI can also play a pivotal role in personal finance. Tools like Mint, YNAB (You Need a Budget), and Personal Capital analyze spending patterns, provide insights on saving, and recommend strategies to achieve financial goals. Investment apps like Betterment and Wealthfront use AI to optimize portfolios based on individual risk tolerance and market trends.

Wellness and Self-Care Assistants. AI tools are also transforming wellness and mental health management. Apps like Headspace and Calm offer guided meditation and stress-relief exercises tailored to user needs, while AI-driven health apps like MyFitnessPal and Fitbit provide personalized recommendations for fitness and nutrition. For mental health support, platforms like Woebot use conversational AI to offer emotional support and coping strategies.

Creative Exploration Tools. For individuals seeking to explore creativity, AI-powered tools like DALL·E, MidJourney, and RunwayML generate visual art, music, or video concepts, inspiring users to push creative boundaries. These tools can help artists and creators brainstorm ideas, experiment with new styles, and enhance their projects with minimal effort.

Making Art and Visual Content. AI is unlocking new possibilities in visual creativity. Tools like DALL·E, MidJourney, and RunwayML allow artists to generate stunning visuals, illustrations, or designs based on simple text prompts. For example, an artist could describe a "surreal underwater city illuminated by bioluminescent creatures," and the AI will create a unique image based on that idea. These tools are not just for professionals; they make artistic expression accessible to anyone, regardless of skill level. Designers and marketers also use platforms like Canva to create visually appealing graphics with AI-powered templates and suggestions.

Composing Music and Audio Content. AI tools like AIVA and Amper Music allow users to compose original music tailored to specific moods or genres. Musicians can use these platforms to create backing tracks, experiment with new sounds, or generate inspiration for their compositions. Podcasters and video creators can also benefit from tools like Descript, which offers AI-powered audio editing, transcription, and even voice cloning, streamlining the production process.

Producing Videos and Animations. AI-powered platforms like Synthesia and Pictory make video creation easier than ever. Users can create professional-looking videos using virtual avatars or automated editing tools without needing advanced video production skills. For animators, tools like RunwayML assist in generating and refining animations, opening doors to faster and more accessible content production.

Generating Innovative Business Ideas. Entrepreneurs can use AI tools like ChatGPT or Copy.ai to brainstorm business ideas, create marketing copy, or even develop a business plan. These tools analyze market trends and consumer behavior to suggest unique approaches to solving problems, helping businesses stand out in competitive markets.

Expanding Educational Horizons. In addition to traditional AI learning platforms like Coursera and Khan Academy, tools like ChatGPT can act as personal tutors, answering questions and explaining complex topics in a conversational way. For instance, students learning coding or mathematics can ask for clarifications, examples, or step-by-step guides tailored to their pace and understanding.

Enhancing Photography and Video Editing. AI tools like Adobe Photoshop and Luminar AI simplify photo and video editing with features like automated background removal, color grading, and object recognition. Creators can enhance images, restore old photos, or experiment with artistic filters effortlessly, saving hours of manual work.

Building Interactive Stories and Games. AI is enabling individuals to create interactive content, such as games or stories. Platforms like Inklewriter and ChatGPT allow users to design branching narratives for games or choose-your-own-adventure stories. Game developers can also use AI engines like Unity ML-Agents to create smarter non-player characters (NPCs) or enhance gameplay dynamics.

By leveraging these AI tools, individuals can break creative barriers, explore new hobbies, or elevate their professional projects. Whether writing a novel, composing music, designing visuals, or launching a business, AI empowers users to unlock their full potential and achieve goals that once seemed out of reach.

To integrate AI into your daily routine for maximum benefit, start by identifying repetitive or time-consuming tasks that AI can streamline. Use AI-powered tools like **Google Calendar** or **Todoist** to manage your schedule, set reminders, and prioritize tasks effectively. For writing and communication, tools like **Grammarly** or **ChatGPT** can help draft emails, reports, or creative content quickly and professionally. Incorporate AI into personal development by using platforms like **Duolingo** for language learning or **Khan Academy** for academic skills. Additionally, leverage AI tools like **MyFitnessPal** or **Fitbit** to track health and fitness goals, or AI assistants like **Siri** and **Alexa** to automate smart home devices. Regularly review and customize these tools to ensure they align with your evolving needs, and balance automation with personal interaction to maintain a human touch in your daily activities.

16. Creating a Balanced Relationship with AI

Human + AI. As AI tools become increasingly integrated into our personal and professional lives, it's essential to create a balanced relationship that leverages the strengths of both humans and machines. While AI excels at processing vast amounts of data, identifying patterns, and automating repetitive tasks, it cannot replicate the depth of human intuition and creativity. These uniquely human traits play a crucial role in areas where emotional intelligence, ethical judgment, and innovative thinking are required.

Human intuition is vital for making decisions in complex or ambiguous situations where AI may fall short. For example, while AI can analyze trends and predict outcomes based on historical data, it lacks the contextual understanding and emotional awareness to fully assess the nuances of a situation. In fields like leadership, counseling, or creative problem-solving, human judgment often relies on instincts, empathy, and cultural sensitivity that AI cannot emulate.

Similarly, creativity is an area where humans continue to outperform AI. While AI tools like DALL·E or ChatGPT can generate ideas or assist with creative tasks, the original vision and emotional resonance of truly impactful work come from human experience and imagination. For instance, an artist might use AI to explore visual concepts but relies on their creative instincts to refine those ideas into meaningful art. This synergy between human creativity and AI's efficiency leads to innovative outcomes that neither could achieve alone.

Maintaining this balance also requires being mindful of over-reliance on AI. While AI tools can boost productivity and solve problems, it's important to remain engaged and critical of the results they produce. For example, professionals using AI in hiring or content creation must regularly evaluate outputs for biases or inaccuracies, ensuring that human oversight guides the process.

By combining human intuition and creativity with the precision and speed of AI tools, we can foster a collaborative dynamic where technology enhances, rather than replaces, human potential. This balanced approach ensures that we use AI responsibly and effectively, while preserving the qualities that make us uniquely human.

Managing Screen Time and Practicing Digital Wellness. Maintaining a healthy balance between technology use and personal well-being is crucial. Managing screen time and practicing digital wellness ensures that we benefit from AI without letting it dominate our daily routines or impact our mental and physical health.

- Set Boundaries for Technology Use. To prevent overuse, establish clear boundaries for when and how you interact with AI tools and screens. For example, set specific times to check emails or use productivity apps, and designate tech-free zones, like the bedroom or dining table, to create space for relaxation and meaningful connections. Many AI tools, like Apple Screen Time or Digital Wellbeing by Google, help track your device usage and set daily limits, ensuring you stay mindful of your screen time.

- Schedule Regular Breaks. Prolonged screen use can lead to fatigue and decreased focus. Incorporate the Pomodoro Technique, which alternates periods of focused work with short breaks, to avoid burnout. AI-powered productivity tools like Focus Booster or Forest can help you manage this schedule while staying productive. During breaks, step away from screens entirely – stretch, go for a walk, or engage in an offline hobby to recharge.
- Prioritize Meaningful Activities. While AI can optimize tasks and provide entertainment, it's important to allocate time for activities that nurture personal growth and relationships. Use AI to free up time by automating repetitive tasks, but reinvest that time into pursuing hobbies, spending time with loved ones, or engaging in mindfulness practices. For instance, use AI fitness apps like Fitbit to track workouts but ensure you also enjoy outdoor exercise for fresh air and real-world interaction.
- Practice Mindful Technology Use. Be intentional about your interactions with AI and digital devices. Avoid multitasking with multiple screens and instead focus on using one tool or app at a time. Turn off unnecessary notifications to reduce distractions and regain control over your attention. Apps like Jumbo

Privacy or Freedom can block distracting websites and help you stay present during work or leisure.

- Reflect on Your Technology Habits. Regularly assess how AI and digital tools impact your life. Are they saving you time, or are they consuming it? Are they enhancing your well-being or causing stress? Use AI tools like RescueTime to analyze how you spend your screen time and adjust your habits to align with your personal goals.

By setting boundaries, prioritizing meaningful activities, and practicing mindful usage, you can maintain a healthy relationship with AI and technology. This balanced approach allows you to enjoy the benefits of AI while preserving your mental clarity, physical health, and overall well-being.

Responsible and Mindful Use of AI. AI offers incredible opportunities to enhance productivity, creativity, and convenience, but it also comes with challenges like privacy risks, ethical concerns, and the potential for over-reliance. By approaching AI with intention and awareness, we can harness its benefits while minimizing its drawbacks.

Responsible AI use begins with understanding its capabilities and limitations. While AI excels at automating tasks and processing large datasets, it's not perfect. Mistakes, biases, and inaccuracies can occur, particularly if the data behind an AI system is flawed. Users should critically evaluate AI outputs and apply human judgment, especially in high-stakes situations like hiring, healthcare, or financial decisions. By remaining informed and questioning AI-generated results, we can prevent potential harm and ensure that technology serves as a helpful tool rather than a source of unintended consequences.

Mindful use of AI also involves respecting privacy and data security. Many AI systems rely on personal data to function effectively, but this data should be shared thoughtfully and only with trusted platforms. Review privacy settings, limit unnecessary data sharing, and use tools that prioritize user control and transparency. Being proactive about protecting your information helps ensure that AI is used ethically and aligns with your personal values.

Finally, balance is key to using AI mindfully. While AI can save time and effort, it's important not to let technology dominate your life. Set boundaries for screen time, prioritize face-to-face interactions, and use AI to complement, rather than replace, human connection and creativity. For example, AI can help generate ideas or streamline tasks, but the final vision and decision-making should remain firmly in human hands. By using AI responsibly and mindfully, we can maximize its potential to improve our lives while upholding ethical standards and maintaining our humanity. This balanced approach allows us to embrace AI as a tool for progress without losing sight of the values and relationships that matter most.

Conclusion: Empowering the Human in the AI Era

As this book comes to an end, below is a summery of some of the main key takeaways:

1. Understanding AI Made Simple

AI is not just for experts; it's becoming a part of everyone's daily life. From chatbots to smart assistants, understanding how AI works empowers you to use it effectively. The book demystifies AI concepts, showing how tools like machine learning and natural language processing shape industries and everyday interactions.

2. Adapting to Change with Confidence

AI is transforming workplaces by automating tasks, creating new opportunities, and reshaping existing roles. Embrace adaptability by learning skills that complement AI, such as creativity, critical thinking, and emotional intelligence. The book highlights practical ways to pivot careers and thrive alongside AI advancements.

3. Lifelong Learning is Essential

Continuous education is the key to staying relevant in the AI era. The book provides resources like online courses, AI-powered learning platforms, and real-world projects to help readers acquire in-demand skills, from coding to data literacy. Emphasis is placed on building technical and soft skills to succeed in a dynamic world.

4. AI in Education and Daily Life

AI enhances learning by personalizing educational experiences and providing access to new tools. It also simplifies daily life by automating tasks, improving productivity, and creating smarter home environments. Readers are encouraged to leverage AI for growth while maintaining an awareness of its limits.

5. **Navigating Ethical and Societal Challenges**

The book explores the double-edged sword of AI, addressing issues like job displacement, bias, surveillance, and misinformation. By promoting ethical AI practices and engaging in conversations about policy and advocacy, readers can contribute to a future where AI is used responsibly.

6. **Balance is the Key to Thriving**

While AI offers immense convenience, maintaining a balanced relationship with technology is crucial. The book emphasizes mindful AI use, including setting boundaries for screen time, protecting personal data, and prioritizing human connection and creativity over digital reliance.

7. **A Call to Action: Empower Yourself**

Adapting to AI isn't just about survival—it's an opportunity for growth. By understanding and embracing AI, learning new skills, and staying adaptable, readers can not only thrive in the AI era but also help shape its ethical and equitable integration into society.

AI and You equips readers with the knowledge, tools, and mindset needed to navigate the rapidly evolving AI landscape, emphasizing that adaptability, lifelong learning, and balance are the cornerstones of success in this transformative era.

The era of AI is not something to fear—it's an opportunity to grow, innovate, and shape the future. Whether you're learning a new skill, exploring how AI tools can make your life easier, or engaging in conversations about AI's impact on society, the first step is always the most important. Start small: take an online course, experiment with an AI tool, or simply learn how AI already affects your daily life. Remember, you don't have to be an expert to thrive in this new era—what matters is your willingness to adapt and learn. Embrace the possibilities, stay curious, and take charge of your journey with AI. The future is here, and it's waiting for you to step into it with confidence and purpose.

Below you can find curated resources for further Exploration

Books

1. "AI Superpowers: China, Silicon Valley, and the New World Order" by Kai-Fu Lee

   o A thought-provoking analysis of AI's global impact and the competition between China and the U.S. in AI innovation.

2. "Life 3.0: Being Human in the Age of Artificial Intelligence" by Max Tegmark

   o Explores the future of AI and its potential impact on society, ethics, and humanity.

3. "Prediction Machines: The Simple Economics of Artificial Intelligence" by Ajay Agrawal, Joshua Gans, and Avi Goldfarb

   o Offers a straightforward perspective on how AI can transform decision-making and businesses.

4. "The Alignment Problem: Machine Learning and Human Values" by Brian Christian

   o Discusses the challenges of ensuring AI aligns with human goals and values.

5. "Human Compatible: Artificial Intelligence and the Problem of Control" by Stuart Russell

   o Examines the risks and ethical dilemmas posed by AI and how to address them.

Websites and Online Platforms

1. Coursera (coursera.org)

   o Offers a variety of AI-related courses, such as "AI For Everyone" by Andrew Ng.

2. Google AI Education (ai.google/education)

   o Free resources and tutorials to learn AI and machine learning basics.

3. Kaggle (kaggle.com)

   o Provides datasets, competitions, and micro-courses for hands-on AI learning.

4. Microsoft Learn (learn.microsoft.com)

   o Offers AI fundamentals and tutorials on Azure AI services.

5. AI Ethics Institute (aiethicsinstitute.org)

   o A resource hub for learning about the ethical implications of AI.

Courses

1. "Machine Learning" by Stanford University (Andrew Ng)

   o Available on Coursera; a foundational course covering algorithms and applications.

2. "AI For Everyone" by Andrew Ng

   o A beginner-friendly introduction to AI, also on Coursera.

3. "Elements of AI" by the University of Helsinki (elementsofai.com)

   o Free, accessible courses designed to teach the basics of AI to anyone.

4. DeepLearning.AI Specializations (deeplearning.ai)

   o Includes in-depth courses on deep learning, natural language processing, and machine learning.

5. "Data Science and Machine Learning Bootcamp" by Udemy

   o Affordable, practical training on AI and data science tools like Python and TensorFlow.

Podcasts

1. "The AI Alignment Podcast"

   o Discusses technical and philosophical challenges of aligning AI with human values.

2. "The TWIML AI Podcast"

   o Features interviews with AI practitioners, researchers, and innovators.

3. "In Machines We Trust"

   o Explores the implications of AI and automation in daily life.

Communities and Forums

1. Reddit AI Communities

   o Subreddits like r/MachineLearning and r/ArtificialIntelligence offer active discussions and resources.

2. Stack Overflow

o   A go-to platform for coding questions, including AI and machine learning topics.

3. AI-focused Meetups (meetup.com)

    o   Find local or virtual events to network and learn from AI enthusiasts and experts.

These resources provide a starting point for anyone interested in exploring AI, whether you're a beginner looking to understand the basics or a professional aiming to deepen your expertise. Dive in and take the next step in your AI journey!

www.ingramcontent.com/pod-product-compliance
Lightning Source LLC
LaVergne TN
LVHW051747050326
832903LV00029B/2773